A souvenir guide

Newark Park
Gloucestershire

yntz and the   2
nd tenants
Park

Tour of the House   10
11 East Front
11 South Front
11 West and North Fronts
12 Entrance Hall
12 Garden Hall
12 Drawing Room
13 Dining Room
13 Stairs
13 First-floor Landing
14 Central Gallery
14 Tudor Bedroom
15 Swan Bedroom
15 Georgian Bedroom
15 Gallery Room
15 Basement

Garden and Park   16
17 Walled Garden
17 Pleasure Grounds
17 Lake and Summerhouse
17 Park

Bibliography   18

National Trust

On the edge

Newark Park stands tall on top of the Cotswold escarpment, looking down into the Ozleworth Valley. This remote corner of south Gloucestershire is a secret and unspoilt place, with barely a sign of modern life visible in any direction.

From Tudor to Neo-classical

The house was built around 1550 for the Tudor courtier Sir Nicholas Poyntz as a hunting lodge. From the roof he could watch the chase in the deer-park below. In the 1670s Sir Gabriel Lowe doubled the size of the house by adding the west range. Newark achieved its present appearance in the 1790s, when it was remodelled for the Rev. Lewis Clutterbuck in a Neo-classical style, probably by the fashionable architect James Wyatt. It remained in the same family (although rented out from 1860) until 1949, when it was bequeathed to the National Trust. The Trust let out the house, but did not look after it.

Rescue

The turning-point came in 1970 with the arrival of Robert Parsons, who spent the rest of his life remaking the derelict house and garden. His energy, imagination and money transformed Newark Park into the warm and welcoming home you see today.

Good food and interesting guests
'What Parsons made of his impressive hill-top eyrie was a unique place of hospitality, one of aristocratic largesse and democratic openness. It was in this latter quality that his American side showed itself so attractively; Newark in his hands became a social centre for a fairly isolated corner of the Cotswolds.'
Charles Tomlinson on Robert Parsons

Sir Nicholas Poyntz and the 'Newe Worke'

IE OBAIS A QVI IE DOIS
IE SERS A QVI ME PLAIST
ET SVIS A QVI ME MERIT

In 1527 Nicholas Poyntz married Joan Berkeley, from one of the most powerful Catholic families in Gloucestershire. However, Poyntz himself was an evangelical Protestant, and a loyal courtier and soldier who supported Henry VIII's marriage to the Protestant Anne Boleyn in 1553. In August 1535 he invited Henry and Anne to stay at his country home twelve miles from Newark at Acton Court, which was lavishly redecorated for the occasion with ornate Renaissance murals, Italian maiolica and Venetian glass. When nearby Kingswood Abbey, which had owned the Ozleworth estate since the 13th century, was dissolved in 1538, Poyntz exploited his royal connections to acquire it. The demolished abbey also provided Poyntz with stone for the construction of Newark Park about 1550.

A grand grandstand

The 'Newe Worke', as it was called, comprised four storeys: a basement kitchen and servants' quarters, ground-floor reception rooms, a large banqueting room on the first floor, and bedrooms on the second floor. The building seems to have been designed primarily as a grandstand, from which to watch deer being hunted in the valley below, although the 17th-century antiquary John Aubrey suggested that Poyntz built Newark 'to keep his whores in'.

Whether he meant the building for sport or sex, he did not enjoy it for long, as he died in 1556 deep in debt and facing charges arising from his involvement in the Dudley conspiracy against Mary Tudor. The house passed to his widow Joan, who lived here until she remarried. Dame Joan's old age was blighted by a cruel second husband and by illness which so touched Queen Elizabeth that she paid her medical bills.

Page 4

Left Sir Nicholas Poyntz (c.1510–56), builder of Newark Park; painted by Hans Holbein (Ickworth). He is wearing the gold chain given him by the King when he was knighted (probably in 1535)

Above right An artist's impression of Tudor Newark Park, which survives today as the east front. The rooftop viewing platform originally seems to have had a balustrade and little domed banqueting houses at the corners, somewhat similar to Sharington's tower at Lacock Abbey

Below right The 16th-century weather vane features a gilded dragon

Page 5 The east front has changed little since Tudor times

Later owners and tenants

The Lowes

In 1572 Newark was bought by Sir Thomas Rivet, a London merchant, whose daughter Alice sold it to Sir Thomas Lowe in 1593. Lowe was another prosperous City merchant, who was much involved, as Governor of the Levant Company, in trade with the eastern Mediterranean, exporting Gloucestershire cloth and importing silk, spices and other exotic goods. His eldest son and heir, Sir Gabriel Lowe, enlarged the house in the mid-17th century, by adding a matching block on the west side of the Poyntz building, which was linked to it by a now-lost central staircase to form an H plan. On the top floor Sir Gabriel also inserted a barrel-ceilinged long gallery running north-south, which is still partly visible.

Like Poyntz, the Lowe family got into debt and were obliged to sell the estate in 1722.

The Clutterbucks

James Clutterbuck, who bought Newark in 1769, was a London cloth-merchant and banker with local connections, and a friend and financial adviser to the actor-manager David Garrick, whom he helped to acquire the Drury Lane theatre. Garrick gratefully repaid him by recommending remedies for piles. Clutterbuck had no children, and so bequeathed Newark to his first cousin, the Rev. Lewis Clutterbuck, who became rector of Ozleworth. The Rev. Clutterbuck commissioned a thorough modernisation of the house around 1790 (the date of his first marriage), probably from the leading London architect James Wyatt. There is no documentary evidence for Wyatt's involvement, which is first recorded only in 1825, in Brewer's *Delineations of Gloucestershire*, but Clutterbuck's son was still alive at the time and presumably would have been able to verify the attribution. Wyatt was certainly working in the area in the 1790s, but was both busy and disorganised, and so is unlikely to have been closely involved. Externally, Clutterbuck's architect emphasized the house's ancient history, adding battlements to the roofline and a Gothick portico to the new south front overlooking the best views. Inside, the changes were more radical and classical. The highlight is the new central hall, which is divided by a screen of columns.

Newark remained in the hands of the Clutterbuck family, but they rented out the house from about 1860. From 1898 it was leased by Mrs Annie King, the widow of a wealthy Bristol shipping agent, Richard Pool King. She gave new life to the place, adding a servants' wing to the north side of the house and bringing up their five children here. Thomas King was a prominent figure in local hunting and racing circles. Mary was a keen gardener, who replanted the walled garden and created the woodland garden. The youngest daughter, Alice, lived on in the house till her death in 1949, when it was given to the National Trust by Mrs Catherine Annie Power-Clutterbuck in memory of her son James, who had been killed in 1917 while serving with the Royal Flying Corps.

The National Trust let the house to a succession of tenants, who converted it into a nursing home, but the building rapidly declined in institutional use, and the garden ran to seed.

'She was very much a lady of her generation, social class and upbringing, courteous and kind, but not to be trifled with. … always dressed in black and wearing a hat.'

Catherine Annie (d.1957), the last of the Clutterbucks

'The general effect induced is one of Wagnerian desolation and unrelieved gloom … on the whole little can be said for the house.'

James Lees-Milne, the National Trust's first Historic Buildings Secretary, 1949

From left to right

The City merchant Sir Thomas Lowe, who bought the Ozleworth estate in 1593 and whose son Gabriel rebuilt Newark Park

The Rev. Lewis Clutterbuck's coat of arms appears in the painted glass on the Staircase Landing. The glass was restored in 1984–5 with money from the Alec Clifton-Taylor bequest

The Rev. Lewis Clutterbuck commissioned the Neo-classical redecoration of the house in the 1790s

Mary King in the Walled Garden in the late 19th century

Saving Newark Park

Newark Park flourishes today very largely thanks to one man: Robert Parsons.

Parsons was born in Oklahoma in 1920, but was raised in Wichita Falls, Texas, and never lost his Texas drawl. He first came to Britain during the Second World War with the US Army 65th Fighter Wing. Stationed in East Anglia, he fell in love with England's ancient buildings and the English way of life. After the war he studied architecture at Harvard, but returned to Britain in 1950, settling in East Anglia where he restored a 16th-century cottage. He later moved to London, becoming a successful antique dealer and property developer in an artistic circle that included the stage designer Leslie Hurry.

In 1970 a friend who knew that he was looking for an old country house to restore pointed him towards Newark Park. Although the house was then in a desperate state, Parsons immediately saw its potential and

took on the tenancy. A huge amount of expensive repair work was needed to make Newark's ancient fabric watertight and secure. He then set about redecorating and refurnishing the interior in his own personal style, which was an eclectic mixture of the ancient and modern, western and eastern, quirky and conventional. He performed similar miracles in the overgrown garden.

Bob Parsons not only rescued Newark, but made it a welcoming place of good food and good company. His wide circle of friends included the Duchess of Westminster and the local postman. However, in 1993 he was diagnosed with Parkinson's disease and decided to give up the tenancy. In fact, he turned out to be suffering from a brain tumour, which was successfully removed, and so he was able to return to the house he had done so much to save. He died here in 2000.

Above Robert Parsons in the park at Newark with Trudy; painted by Robert Collins

Left Robert Parsons rescued the derelict summerhouse

Right The Georgian Bedroom is one of the new interiors created by Robert Parsons

Tour of the House

The Exterior

Far left The South and
East Fronts

Left The Gothick porch on
the South Front

Below The North Front

The East Front

Faced with finely cut, locally quarried
limestone, this has changed very little since
it was built about 1550. It retains its
Renaissance symmetry, with a central bay
window over two floors. The doorcase has
fluted Doric columns, and a (recarved)
roundel in the pediment bears the Poyntz
arms. It is a very early example of the classical
style in England, but was probably moved
here when another front was rebuilt.
The battlements were added in the 1790s.
The National Trust restored the leaded
lights in 1984.

The South Front

This was rebuilt in the 1790s on the brink
of the cliff with a semi-octagonal Gothick
porch offering superb views over the
new deer-park. The sash-windows on
the right-hand side are false for the sake
of symmetry.

The West and North Fronts

These were also rebuilt in the 1790s.
The two-storey servants' wing was added
to the North Front in 1897.

Right The classical doorway
on the East Front

The Interior Ground Floor & Staircase

The Entrance Hall

This impressive Neo-classical space was cut out of the centre of the house in the 1790s. It has been repainted following the late 18th-century scheme. The painted pine entrance door carefully follows the curve of the semi-circular apse. The matching apse at the far end has niches for sculpture. A central screen of Doric columns divides the room, which is enlivened by a frieze of *bucrania* (ox skulls), swags and garlands. The grille in the Dining Room doorway was installed in 1898 as part of a new hot-air central heating system.

The Garden Hall

Your eye is drawn irresistibly to the window, which offers one of the most impressive views in Gloucestershire, south-west to the Mendips. The frieze is 18th-century, the wall-panelling probably 19th-century. The 18th-century decoration has been reinstalled.

The Drawing Room

You now enter the mid-17th-century west range, which was comprehensively remodelled in the 1790s, when the frieze was put up. Bob Parsons installed the 18th-century *fireplace* in the 1970s.

Furniture and ceramics

The huge 18th-century mahogany *bookcase* against the far wall is the only piece of furniture to survive from the Clutterbuck era, when it stood in the Smoking Room (now the Kitchen). It is now used to display an impressive collection of *Staffordshire figures* bequeathed by Harvey and Joyce Churchward.

Flanking the fireplace is a pair of amboyna-wood *writing-desks* (on loan from Ightham Mote).

Left **The Garden Hall**

Above **The bookcase in the Drawing Room displays a fine collection of Staffordshire figures**

Right **The wallpaper on the Dining Room ceiling was designed by William Morris in 1881**

Below right **The Dining Room**

Far right **The 16th-century bay window on the Staircase Landing is filled with late 18th-century painted glass**

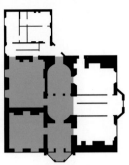

The Dining Room

This room was also created in the 1790s, but the William Morris wallpaper was put up on the ceiling by the King family in 1898, when they were leasing the house. Parsons added both the fireplace and the bookshelves in the 1990s, when he was using this as a living room.

Pictures

Hanging over the mantelpiece is a portrait of Bob Parsons in the garden with his Great Dane, which was painted by Rob Collins, a local Gloucestershire artist. Collins also painted the East Front with Parsons and his partner, Michael Claydon, who worked on the project from 1982. Flanking the fireplace are large semi-abstract landscapes by Christopher P. Wood. Over the door is an Aboriginal dot painting by the Warlayisti artist Sidney Morris.

The Stairs

The Staircase is contemporary with the 1790s Entrance Hall from which it rises at right-angles; The first flight is stone, the second wood, with a plain wrought-iron balustrade.

The First-floor Landing

The handsome bay window would originally have lit the banqueting room which occupied the whole of the first floor of the Tudor east range. The leaded lights are filled with late 18th-century painted glass, including the coat of arms of the Rev. Lewis Clutterbuck, who commissioned the 1790s staircase.

The Interior
Second Floor
& Basement

The Central Gallery

The gallery at the top of the stairs which runs north-south across the centre of the house was created out of two rooms during repair work in the 1970s. Conservation also revealed a 16th-century window and the rubble stonework under later plaster.

From the south window (at the far end) there are spectacular panoramic views east to the Marlborough Downs, south to the Mendips and west to Bristol.

The Tudor Bedroom

The original 16th-century fireplace and small garderobe chamber (lavatory) emerged during restoration. Bob Parsons commissioned the painted decoration of the fireplace wall, which was inspired by the famous early 17th-century painted panelling in the Long Gallery at Powis Castle in Powys.

Picture

Over the bed hangs a 19th-century copy of *A Satyr mourning over a Nymph* by Piero di Cosimo (1462–1521) in the National Gallery. The engravings are by the German Renaissance artist Martin Schongauer and others.

Above right A bowl of pot-pourri in the Tudor Bedroom fireplace

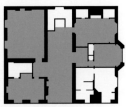

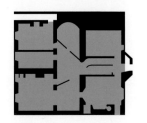

The Swan Bedroom

The room takes its name from the white swans collected by Bob Parsons over many years. The outer doorframe is 16th-century.

The Georgian Bedroom

This room originally formed the south end of the 17th-century long gallery. The tent-like ceiling was put up in the 1970s and painted to resemble bleached wood.

The Gallery Room

This retains the barrel-vaulted ceiling of the Long Gallery which occupied the entire top floor of the 17th-century west range. It also still has its original hand-sawn elm floorboards.

The room is used today for changing exhibitions about Newark Park, its history and collections.

Retrace your steps to the ground floor, leave the house and walk round to the West Front, and step in through a window to basement rooms.

The Basement

These were the servants' quarters, comprising kitchen, servants' hall, bakehouse, wine cellar, dairy, pantry and scullery. Modern RSJs have had to be inserted to support subsiding floors, and most of the furnishings have disappeared, but otherwise these atmospheric spaces have changed very little. The 16th-century Kitchen still has its original Tudor fireplace arch, set into walls almost two metres thick and flanked by ovens. A Tudor serving hatch also survives in the rubble-stone wall opposite, which is the only unaltered internal partition to remain.

Far left **The Central Gallery**

Above **The Tudor Bedroom**

Left **The Gallery Room**

The Garden and Park